D0712595

The Bionic Hand

by Adam Woog

Norwood House Press
PO Box 316598
Chicago, Illinois 60631

For information regarding Norwood House Press, please visit our Web site at:

www.norwoodhousepress.com or call 866-565-2900.

Acknowledgments:
My thanks to Phil Newman of Touch Bionics for his research help.

LIBRARY OF CONGRESS CATALOGING-IN-PUBLICATION DATA

Woog, Adam, 1953–
The bionic hand / Adam Woog.
   p. cm. — (A great idea)
Summary: "Explores the development and creation of the i-LIMB which is the
first commercially available bionic hand"—Provided by publisher.
Includes bibliographical references and index.
ISBN-13: 978-1-59953-341-4 (lib. ed. : alk. paper)
ISBN-10: 1-59953-341-3 (lib. ed. : alk. paper) 1. Artificial hands—Juvenile
literature. 2. Bionics—Juvenile literature. I. Title.
RD756.22.W66 2009
617.5'75—dc22

2009015640

Manufactured in the United States of America.

Contents

Note: Words that are **bolded** in the text are defined in the glossary on page 45.

Chapter 1

The Idea

"This is Star Wars. This is the future, and I'm wearing it right now."
—Juan Arredondo, U.S. Army Sergeant (Ret.) and i-LIMB Hand user

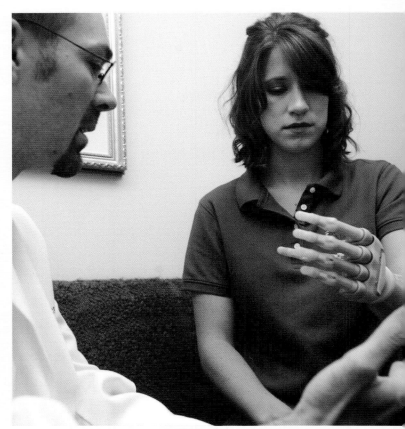

Lindsay Block is fitted with her new i-LIMB Hand.

Lindsay Block lives in Oklahoma. She was born missing her left hand and the lower part of that arm. Lindsay got her first artificial hand when she was only six months old. As her body grew, she got new ones. Meanwhile, the technology to make artificial hands got better. Lindsay's devices became easier to use and control.

But making a machine that imitates a real hand is very difficult. The challenges in building them are huge. So even the best artificial hands were heavy and uncomfortable, and they could make only very simple movements.

Then Lindsay got an amazing new device. It is called the i-LIMB Hand, but its nickname is the Bionic Hand. It is by far the most useful and lifelike hand she has ever had. Lindsay says that she is pretty sure that someone who just met her would not guess that it was not her own.

Part Human, Part Machine

Lindsay's hand is the product of a special branch of science. This is bionics. It is the science of combining biology with technology. One part of bionics concentrates on developing artificial limbs. A replacement part like an artificial hand

The i-LIMB Hand is far more sensitive than previous artificial limbs. Here, Lindsay Block uses the i-LIMB Hand to make a telephone call.

The Bionic Hand cannot exactly imitate a real hand. Still, it is making a big difference for people like Lindsay. They can have better lives and can do things they could never do before.

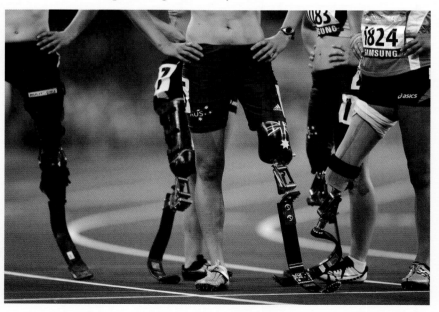

The technology developed for many artificial limbs continues to improve. Here, amputees use specially designed legs to compete in a race.

is called a prosthesis. The science of developing such replacements is called prosthetics.

A person with a prosthesis can be considered as being part machine! In the past, the idea of a human being part machine seemed like science fiction. Now, however, it is no longer just a fantasy. People today can have prosthetic hearts, feet, voice boxes —and hands.

The Complexity of Hands

It is very difficult to build machines that can imitate what the human body can do. This is because every part of the body is extremely complex.

The hand is no exception. It has 27 bones, 22 joints, and 40 muscles (including some muscles that are in the forearm). It also has hundreds of nerves, tendons, and other parts.

All of these parts work together so that the hand can make many complicated movements. For example, humans can use their opposable thumbs.

Opposable thumbs can turn back against the other four fingers of the

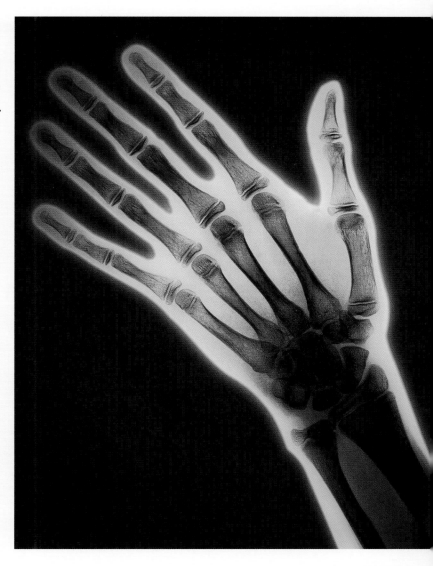

A hand is a particularly difficult body part to duplicate because of its many bones, muscles, and nerves.

Other Creatures

Opposable thumbs (that curve to meet the other fingers) are needed for many jobs that hands do. For example, they are needed for picking up things.

Humans are not the only living things with these useful thumbs. Many animals also have some type of opposable thumb or toe. Among them are primates (including great apes), lemurs, opossums, giant pandas, and koalas. At least two dinosaurs also had opposable thumbs: the birdlike troödon and the tiny bambiraptor.

Opposable thumbs make it possible for this opossum to grasp a limb and crawl along it while hanging upside down.

hand. If thumbs were not opposable, people could not pick up and hold things. Try doing things without using a thumb, and see how difficult it is!

Thanks to opposable thumbs, people can use tools, hold cups, write, and do many other tasks. This ability has been key to how humans have evolved. Being able to use tools and do other things has helped the human race become highly developed.

Signals from the Brain

Movement is not the only thing about hands that is complicated. The way in which the brain tells the hand how to move is also amazingly complex.

The brain uses tiny amounts of electricity to send signals to the hand (and

Did You Know?

About 10,000 people in the United States lose an upper extremity (arm, hand, or finger) each year.

everywhere else in the body) through the nervous system. The signals are called **myoelectric** signals. This kind of signal is very small. It is less than a millionth of the strength of a lightbulb.

When it gets a signal from the brain, the hand reacts. The signals "tell" certain muscles to contract in certain ways. These contractions then make the hand move.

The hand also sends signals to the brain. For example, suppose someone's hand touches a hot stove. Nerves in the skin detect the heat and "tell" the brain.

Right away, the brain sends more signals to the muscles of the hand and arm. These signals then "tell" the muscles to move the hand away from the heat. All of this happens in a split second.

Of course, if the hand does not move away fast enough, there is another signal. It's called pain!

Not Having to Think About It

Jerking the hand back from a hot stove is a simple movement, compared to other things the hand does. But even this relatively simple movement is complicated.

It requires the movement of many nerves, tendons, and muscles. They move both independently and together in very precise ways. Tasks like writing, picking up a cup, opening a door, using tools, or throwing a ball are even more complicated.

Pulling your hand away from a hot pot on the stove is simple and automatic. But it involves a complex interaction between the brain, the nerves, and the muscles.

Star Wars

For many years, people have dreamed about replacing arms, legs, and other body parts with machines. Many science fiction books and movies have used this idea.

For example, in *Star Wars: Episode V—The Empire Strikes Back*, Luke Skywalker loses his hand and gets an artificial one.

Before that, two fictional television shows, *The Six Million Dollar Man* and *The Bionic Woman*, were about injured people who got new body parts that gave them superhuman speed, strength, and eyesight.

The i-LIMB Hand's inner workings are exposed. Until recently, such bionic limbs have only been possible in science fiction.

Curious

Jason Henderson lost both of his hands in an accident, and now he has two Bionic Hands. When he first got them, Jason was worried that people would make fun of him.

But that did not happen. Jason says that almost everybody is just curious about his unusual hands. He feels that most people are more interested in learning about them than anything else.

People with normal hands do not have to think about how complicated it is to do even simple things with them. All of the complicated signals and movements are automatic. They just happen as part of everyday life, and they are taken for granted.

Of course, moving a hand (or another part of the body) cannot be taken for granted by people who have trouble with such movements. They can be difficult or even impossible. And if the hand is missing, some things are obviously very difficult or impossible.

Telling the Hand What to Do

The first artificial hands could not move at all. They were simply "dead" replacements, usually made of wood or plastic. However, researchers now can design and build hands that move.

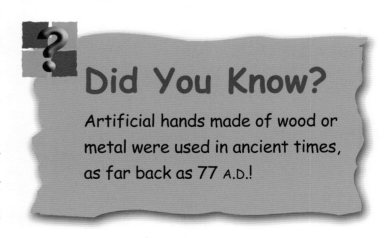

Did You Know?

Artificial hands made of wood or metal were used in ancient times, as far back as 77 A.D.!

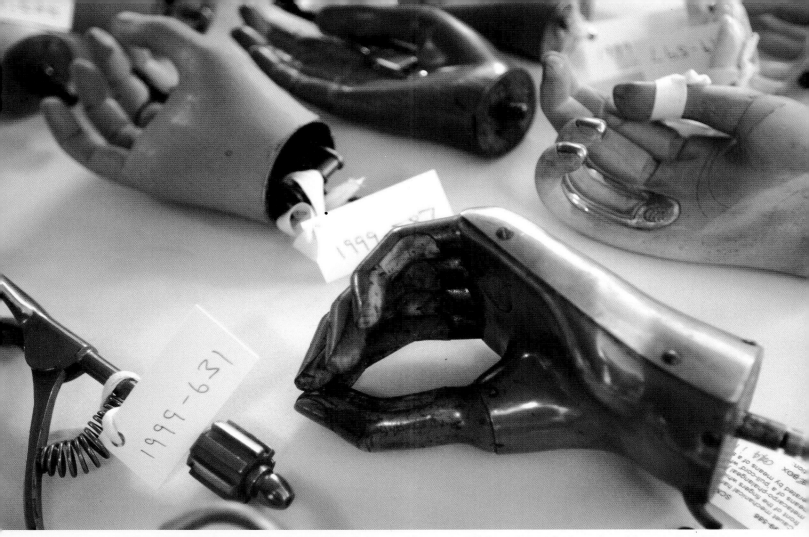

Various prosthetic hands are on display at the Science Museum Object Store in London. Many prostheses are simply models and used only for looks.

It is possible to design these better hands partly because nerves in the arm can still receive myoelectric signals from the brain—and send them to the brain—even if the hand is missing. Sometimes, these signals are a problem. They produce unpleasant "phantom" feelings. It can feel like the hand is still there, even if it is not.

But myoelectric signals can be useful. This is because researchers have found out how to connect an artificial hand to the nerves that are still in the arm.

When the brain sends signals to the arm, the artificial hand picks them up. An amplifier in the hand makes the signals stronger. These signals now have enough power to run tiny computers in the hand. The wearer can then "tell" the hand what to do by flexing certain arm muscles in specific ways.

Learning to use a Bionic Hand is usually easy. This is because it uses the same electrical signals that a real hand does. Some people master it in just a few days, although others might take a few weeks. Raymond Edwards, who was one of the first to use the hand, says that it was easy to learn.

Improving the Artificial Hand

Myoelectric hands are not as advanced as they could be. This is because of the difficulty in imitating the movements of a real hand. Artificial hands are a long way from perfectly imitating real hands.

In fact, most myoelectric hands can only do very simple things, such as making a

Most amputees find the i-LIMB Hand remarkably easy to use. Here, Sgt. Arredondo uses his new i-LIMB Hand to do some shopping.

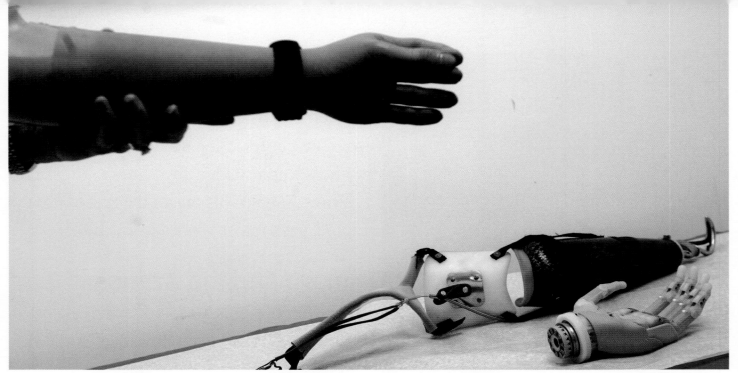

An i-LIMB Hand (bottom right) is shown with a "pincer"-like limb (middle) and a less sophisticated artificial hand (top). The i-LIMB Hand is far more like a real hand, with individual fingers and a functioning opposable thumb.

clawlike pinching movement. Also, they are not easy to control. For example, it is hard to pick up something like a paper cup without crushing it. Furthermore, most myoelectric hands are heavy and uncomfortable.

This is why the i-LIMB Hand is such an amazing invention. It is not the first device to use myoelectric technology. But the researchers who developed the i-LIMB Hand have taken the science to a very high level.

Chapter 2

How It Works

The developer of the i-LIMB Hand, a Scottish company called Touch Bionics, is working to solve the many difficult problems in building a really effective artificial hand. This work requires a complicated mixture of electricity, mechanics, computing, and biology.

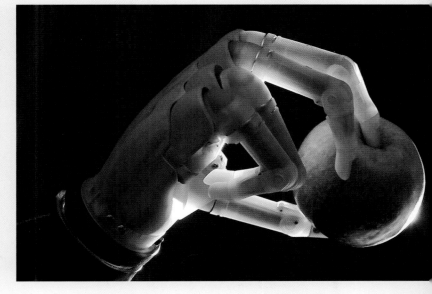

A person with an i-LIMB Hand grasps an apple. Each finger in the i-LIMB Hand is operated by a separate motor, which allows the user to pick up delicate objects without crushing them.

Inspired by Disaster

Research on the i-LIMB Hand began in the 1960s. It was inspired by a terrible medical disaster, caused by a drug (thalidomide) that was popular at the time. The drug was mostly given to pregnant women to help them sleep, but it damaged their babies. About 10,000 babies were born with serious problems, such as missing hands and legs. They needed a lot of help.

In the 1950s, a young boy uses an artificial limb to write. He was born without a lower arm because his mother had been given the drug thalidomide while she was pregnant.

Moving Separate Fingers

A key part in making the i-LIMB Hand work was to perfect how it senses electrical signals. This was needed so that the hand could use the signals to control the arm.

The i-LIMB Hand picks up these signals with two small **electrodes**. These are usually attached to the skin of the arm. When the electrodes pick up the signals, they send them to microprocessors in the hand. The microprocessors then control the motors in each finger.

Older kinds of myoelectric hands pick up signals in similar ways. However, these older hands have only one motor. That means they can only do very simple things.

But each finger of the Bionic Hand has its own motor. So does the wrist. Also, each finger has joints that bend like real

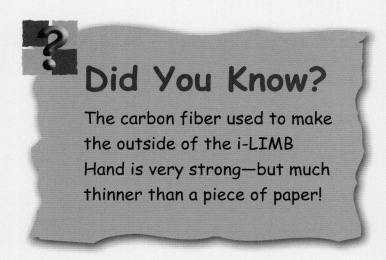

Did You Know?

The carbon fiber used to make the outside of the i-LIMB Hand is very strong—but much thinner than a piece of paper!

joints. So each finger moves by itself, and the wrist rotates. The Bionic Hand can thus make much more complex movements.

Different Movements

A "key grip" is an example of a more complex movement that the i-LIMB Hand can make. This brings the thumb and index finger together. The thumb touches the index finger in the middle of the finger.

Then the hand can hold items such as keys. Because the wrist rotates, users can turn a key in a lock in a normal way.

Another movement is the "power grip." This closes all five fingers toward the middle. It is good for turning doorknobs, or for holding things like cans of soda or coffee cups.

Also, there is the "precision grip." With this, the tips of the index finger, thumb, and middle finger meet. This grip makes it easy to pick up and hold small things, such as coins.

A fourth common position is the "index point." With this movement, every finger closes in a fist except for the index finger. That way, people can use telephones, type on computers, or do other tasks that need just one finger.

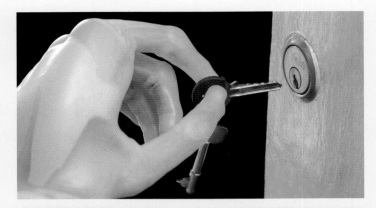

These photographs show the superior grasping and gripping features of the i-LIMB Hand.

And the Bionic Hand can also "park" its thumb. In this movement, the thumb closes against the side of the hand and all

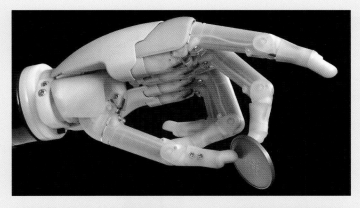

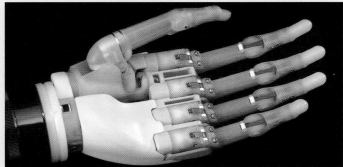

In these pictures, the sensors in the fingers of the i-LIMB Hand can be seen. Like real fingers, these sensors can detect how much pressure is needed to pick up an object.

"Too Much James Bond"

The fingers of the i-LIMB Hand do not just move by themselves. They also automatically sense how much pressure is needed with each of these movements. It does this with a system of sensors in each finger that can detect when they have applied enough pressure. Then the hand automatically stops.

For example, when its user picks up a paper cup, the hand "knows" when to stop closing. The fingers stop gently to avoid crushing the cup. But the Bionic Hand can also grip tightly. It is strong enough to hold heavy things like backpacks or briefcases.

In fact, it is so strong that some people might worry about it. Donald McKillop was the first person in the world to have

of the fingers are held together straight. This makes it easy to do things like taking a jacket on or off.

Donald McKillop was the first person to receive an i-LIMB Hand.

an i-LIMB Hand. He often has to convince people that he is not going to crush their fingers when he shakes hands. In a newspaper article from Scotland, McKillop commented that people "are obsessed by the idea that I . . . could take a tin can and squeeze it into a mangled mess. They've been watching too much James Bond."

Hardware

To create all this movement, the Bionic Hand is made using high-tech hardware. Its moving parts are built with several cutting-edge kinds of metals and plastics. The electronic parts use small and efficient motors and **microprocessors**.

These prosthetic limbs all belong to retired U.S. Army Sergeant Juan Arredondo. Arredondo's i-LIMB Hand is by far the most like a natural hand.

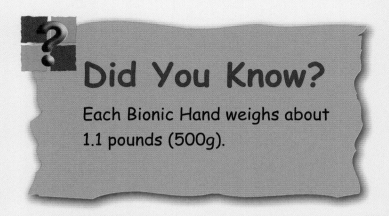

Did You Know?

Each Bionic Hand weighs about 1.1 pounds (500g).

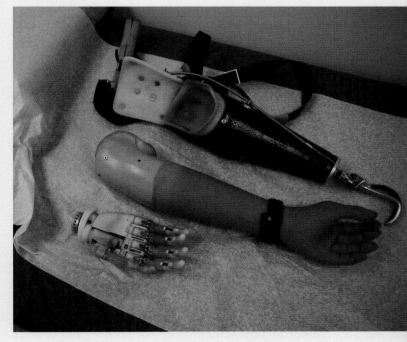

For power, the i-LIMB Hand uses special batteries. They are usually placed on the arm. These are charged overnight. Each charge lasts for a complete day of use.

The hands are built in a basic model. Then they are custom fitted for each person. For example, each hand needs to be molded at the end of the wrist so that it fits comfortably and snugly against the arm.

Another important feature of the i-LIMB Hand's hardware is its **modular** design. This means that it separates easily into smaller pieces. For instance, each finger can be taken off and put back on with just one screw.

This modular design makes repair and adjustment easy. When older styles of hands needed servicing, the whole thing had to be shipped to the maker. The user did not have a hand for several weeks.

Expensive

Right now, an i-LIMB Hand costs many thousands of dollars. The exact price varies a lot. This is because each one has to be customized for the person who will be using it. Some people need a lot of custom work, so it becomes more expensive. But Touch Bionics hopes that its price will drop in the future.

But prosthetics technicians around the world can learn to repair the Bionic Hand. They can repair or adjust it in just a few hours.

RoboCops and Terminators

Some people like to leave the hand uncovered, so that the entire mechanism can be seen. They like how the bare mechanism looks. This has been called "the RoboCop Look" or "the Terminator Look," after two popular movies.

But most of the i-LIMB Hand's users prefer to cover it in a glove of artificial skin. This covering is called LIVINGSKIN. It is very realistic.

LIVINGSKIN is as flexible as real skin. The color and other features can be customized for each person. For example,

Inside the Hand

Some people who wear i-LIMB Hands like to have them look as natural as possible. Others enjoy the way the hands look like robots. The people who like the robot look can have their hands made in black. But they can also get a clear covering that lets people see all of the "guts" of the hand as it works!

An i-LIMB Hand without LIVINGSKIN.

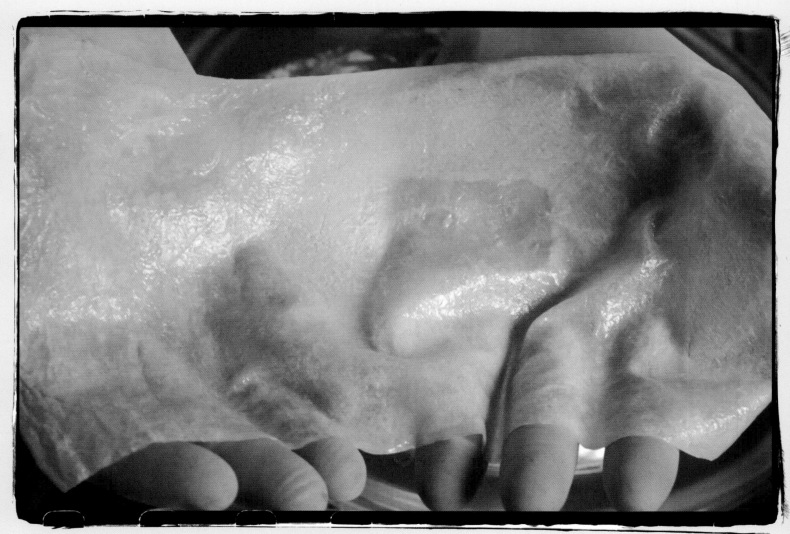

LIVINGSKIN looks and feels much like real skin.

each hand has lifelike touches like wrinkles and blood vessels. In fact, it is difficult to tell the difference in looks between a person's real skin and the artificial skin.

LIVINGSKIN has other advantages. It helps the user grip things better because the skin is not as smooth as bare plastic. Also, it protects the hand from being damaged by dust or water.

Even with the artificial skin, the i-LIMB Hand is not waterproof, so people have to be careful about getting it wet. There is one advantage to this: They do not have to do the dishes!

The Bionic Hand has only been available for a short time. But it has already made a huge difference in the lives of many people.

Lindsay Block holds up both her hands to ask, "Which one is the real hand?" When viewed side by side, the differences between the natural hand on her right and the i-LIMB Hand on her left are barely noticeable.

Chapter 3

Making a Difference

Juan Arredondo shows off the features of his i-LIMB Hand.

The Bionic Hand has helped many people regain their lives. One person whose life has significantly changed is Juan Arredondo of Texas. He is a retired sergeant in the U.S. Army.

In 2004 Sergeant Arredondo was on duty while driving in Iraq when a bomb exploded and he was badly injured. The explosion seriously damaged Juan's

reattach it. However, it was too badly damaged.

Juan returned home to Texas. He had a lot of physical therapy to make his body stronger. In many ways, he recovered well.

A Normal Life

However, his missing hand severely affected Sergeant Arredondo's mental health. He became very depressed. He worried that

legs. It also severed his left arm just below the elbow.

Despite his injuries, Juan remained conscious. He was able to grab his severed hand and forearm.

He kept the limb and put it in his pocket while he was being rescued. He hoped that surgeons would be able to

Did You Know?

About half of the people in the world who have Bionic Hands are from the U.S.

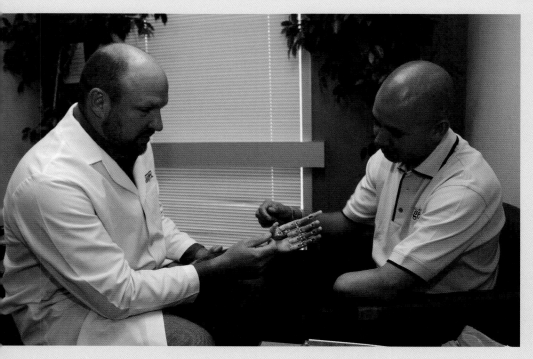

Before being fitted for an i-LIMB Hand, Sgt. Arredondo felt depressed and isolated by the loss of his arm.

program helps wounded veterans adjust to home life.

The prosthetic helped Juan in many practical ways. For example, he can toss a football, drive, or take care of home repairs. He has even done things that can be difficult for people who have both hands, such as whitewater rafting and rock climbing.

he would never be able to lead a normal life. And he was uncomfortable around anyone except close family and friends or other wounded veterans. Juan felt that strangers were staring at him all the time.

But then a special government plan helped him get an i-LIMB Hand. This

Just as important has been the improvement in Sergeant Arredondo's mental health. He is no longer depressed. He is less self-conscious around strangers. He also does not worry about being able to make a

ended his dream of having a career in the military. Evan had especially wanted to become a parachute jumper. Losing his limb also made it much more difficult to play sports, which he had loved.

But then Evan's brother saw a TV report about Touch Bionics. The brother contacted the company. Evan then became one

living for his family. Juan says that his life is much better.

"The Hundreds of Everyday Things You Take for Granted"

Another example of someone whose life has changed because of the i-LIMB Hand is Evan Reynolds. Evan, who lives in England, was a teenager in 2006 when his left hand was severed in a car accident. This

The i-LIMB Hand helps amputees with many simple tasks, such as eating. The i-LIMB Hand's more natural action can help people feel less different.

of the first people in the world to get an i-LIMB Hand. It was an experimental **prototype** of the Bionic Hand.

Evan still cannot join the military, but many other activities are possible. Evan says that he especially appreciates being able to do small things in everyday life. These are things that he never thought about before his accident. He commented in a British newspaper, "People always ask how it's changed my life, but there's no specific thing. It's the hundreds of everyday things you take for

Lindsay Block can participate in normal work activities with the help of her i-LIMB Hand.

granted, which I can do again—like peeling a potato, catching a ball, holding a bottle of water."

He still plays sports often. Evan also loves to do adventurous things like skydiving. However, he does not wear his i-LIMB Hand at such times. He jokes that he would have to be crazy to jump out of a plane with such an expensive hand.

The Bionic Hand has already dramatically changed the lives of people like Evan Reynolds, Lindsay Block, and Juan Arredondo. But it is only the latest in the evolving design of prosthetic hands. In

Playing the Guitar Again

The i-LIMB Hand has made the lives of many people better. Other prosthetics have also made a difference for people. For example, a British rock guitarist, Dorian Cox, had a stroke. His hand was paralyzed. But he was fitted with a mechanical "glove" that fits over his hand. It supports his weakened fingers and responds to electrical signals from his muscles. Now he can play music again.

the future, the i-LIMB Hand will change and improve in many ways.

Chapter 4

Into the Future

Although the Bionic Hand can do much more than other prosthetic hands, it still needs a lot of work. Right now, it can only do a small percentage of what a normal hand can do. Stuart Mead, the head of

Stuart Mead, CEO of Touch Bionics, thinks that technology will continue to improve prosthetic limbs.

Touch Bionics, commented in a magazine article, "A prosthetic doesn't function like a real hand. We're still only able to **replicate** 5 to 10 percent of what a real hand can do."

As technology improves, this ability to reproduce the movement of regular hands will also improve. Prosthetic hands like the i-LIMB Hand will be increasingly easier to use and more **versatile**. Also, the research that goes into improving the Bionic Hand will be used to develop a variety of other myoelectric prosthetics.

Improvements and New Uses

One thing that the researchers at Touch Bionics are exploring is a way to make the i-LIMB Hand in different sizes. Right now, only the i-LIMB Hand's fingers can

Did You Know?

The i-LIMB Hand has won many awards, including being one of *Time* magazine's "fifty best inventions of 2008."

be made in different sizes. The rest of the hand is a one-size-fits-all model.

Of course, an adult-size hand will not work for small children. So Touch Bionics is creating a smaller hand for them. Also, the company is working on a way to make different shapes and sizes for men and women, because their hands are shaped differently.

Touch Bionics is working on developing different-sized i-LIMB Hands so that the hands will be more appropriately sized for women and children.

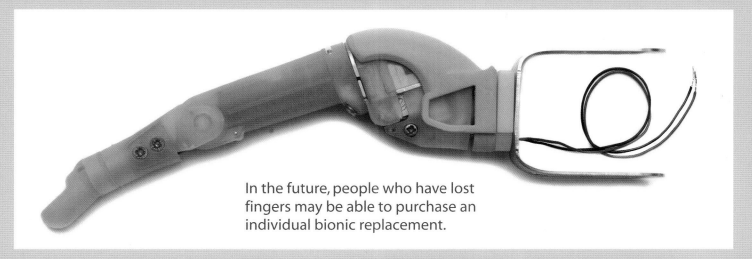

In the future, people who have lost fingers may be able to purchase an individual bionic replacement.

Furthermore, researchers are designing prosthetics for people who are missing only a few fingers. These "bionic fingers" could attach to existing parts of the hand.

Still another project that will be developed is an i-LIMB Hand–style prosthetic for a full arm. Right now, whole artificial arms that use myoelectrics do exist. However, they are not as highly developed or as useful as the i-LIMB Hand.

Other Research Projects

Touch Bionics was the first company to make an articulated myoelectric hand available to the public. However, several other research teams around the world are working on similar projects.

For example, a team in Germany is developing a device called the Fluidhand. It uses a miniature **hydraulic** system. A hydraulic system uses liquid to make things

Helped by Robot Research

Many areas of science will help develop better artificial body parts in the future. One is mechatronics. Mechatronics combines electrical engineering, mechanical engineering, and computers. It is used when creating things like robots.

There are several ways in which mechatronics can help make better prosthetics. For example, research in **robotics** will create smaller, more powerful batteries and motors. These can then be adapted for prosthetics like the Bionic Hand.

A technician shakes hands with a robot while he adjusts its sensors. Many of the technologies for bionic limbs come out of robotic research.

move. In the Fluidhand, tiny chambers are pumped up with fluid to make the fingers move. It was inspired by the way spiders move their legs!

Its inventors say that when it is finished the Fluidhand will have a more natural feel than the i-LIMB Hand. Also, it will be better at closing its fingers around things that have irregular surfaces.

There will be many more kinds of prosthetic hands in the future. But it is important to remember that each person has different needs. Some people may like the i-LIMB Hand best. Others might find another type best. Mead, the head of Touch Bionics, commented in a magazine interview, "Many people have many different devices for different activities, and what works for one patient may not work for another."

A researcher holds a prototype of a thought-controlled arm prosthetic. This prosthetic will actually be wired to a person's nerves and muscles in a complicated surgery so it can be controlled by a user's brain.

Reinnervation

A few years ago, lifelike prosthetic hands seemed like something out of science fiction. Now they are reality. Many of the ideas for future prosthetics are even more amazing. But soon they will be reality, too.

For example, some researchers are working in a field called **targeted muscle reinnervation**. This is a procedure in which a prosthetic is "wired" directly into the user's nervous system to get signals from the brain. This is different from the system used by the i-LIMB Hand, which uses sensors on the skin to pick up the signals.

Reinnervation is not needed for people who are missing a limb below the elbow.

Their arms still have enough muscles to control a prosthetic hand. But people who are missing an arm above the elbow do not have these muscles. Reinnervation will work for them. Nerve endings in their shoulders will control their artificial arms.

A Sense of Touch and More

Another exciting area for future research is **haptic** technology. This is the development of an artificial sense of touch. Right now, prosthetic devices do not have a sense of touch. They cannot send back signals to the brain from the skin. So they cannot sense if something is hot or cold, rough or smooth.

Haptic technology will give artificial limbs this ability. But it is a complicated problem, and it will be difficult to develop. This is because skin is very sensitive. Each square inch of skin has thousands of nerve endings that send signals back to the brain about touch.

The research that is now being done in prosthetic limbs will also help advance the creation of exoskeletons. Exoskeletons are skeletons or shields that are outside the body. An early example of an exoskeleton is the armor that knights wore. A later, fictional example is the suit that the inventor Tony Stark wears in the movie *Iron Man*.

A woman wears an exoskeleton. Currently, such technologies are used by researchers to work in virtual environments. In the future, they may be developed to help people who have had strokes or brain trauma regain movement.

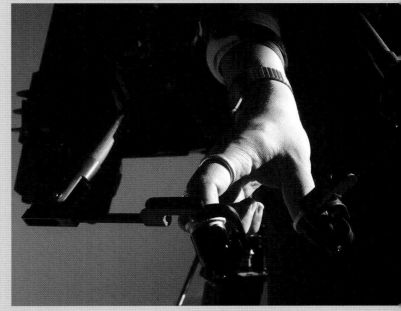

Powered exoskeletons will be able to move on their own, controlled by the wearer's nervous system. These exoskeletons are still being developed. But someday they will greatly help people with physical limitations. For example, people who have suffered strokes are often unable to move one or more of their limbs. But an exoskeleton would support and move the damaged limb.

Cost

Another thing about the i-LIMB Hand that will change over time is its cost. Right now, one hand costs tens of thousands of dollars, depending on how it is customized for specific individuals. This is several times more expensive than a traditional prosthetic hand.

There are many reasons why the Bionic Hand is so expensive. One is that its high-tech materials cost a lot. Also, just like any product, it costs more if only a few are made. But as more people use them, more will be made. The cost will go down.

Of course, making a less expensive i-LIMB Hand will be good for everyone.

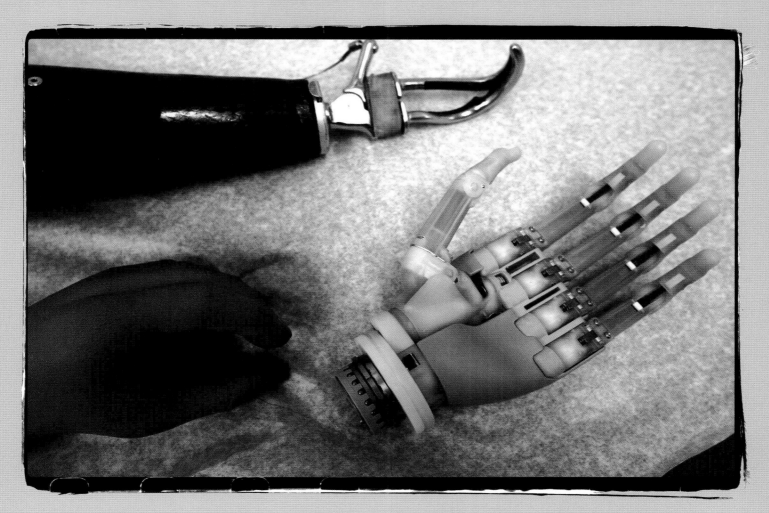

Today, the i-LIMB Hand remains the most significant scientific breakthrough in prosthetic limbs. Scientists continue to try to develop prostheses' function and range to improve the lives of those who have lost limbs.

Plug and Play

The researchers who developed the i-LIMB Hand hope to develop a "plug-and-play" system for prosthetics. This would be like the USB system for computers. It will make connecting parts of prosthetics very easy. For example, separate elbows, hands, shoulders, and wrists would snap together easily.

This will be especially important in parts of the world where many people have lost their limbs because of violent conflicts and war.

Into the Future

No one knows exactly how the Bionic Hand will develop in the future. And no one knows what new ideas will be inspired by it.

However, it is safe to say that future prosthetic limbs will be even smarter, more powerful, and easier to use than they are now. The idea of combining the human body with artificial parts will no longer sound like science fiction. Bionics will be part of everyday life.

Glossary

bionics: The field of science that combines biology, engineering, and technology.

electrodes: Metal devices that can pick up electrical signals.

haptic: Having to do with the sense of touch.

hydraulic: A system that uses liquid to move machinery.

microprocessors: A silicon chip that controls how a computer works.

modular: Able to be easily assembled or disassembled in pieces.

myoelectric: Having to do with the electrical signals sent to muscles by the brain.

prototype: An experimental first version of something.

replicate: To reproduce or make a copy of.

robotics: The technology of designing and building robots.

targeted muscle reinnervation: An experimental procedure in which a prosthetic is "wired" directly into a person's nervous system.

versatile: Able to do many things.

For More Information

Web Sites to Visit

Mark Strassman, "The Little Three-Legged Pony That Could." CBS News, February 23, 2009. (http://www.cbsnews.com/stories/2009/02/23/eveningnews/main4822620.shtml). An article about a horse that was injured and received a prosthetic leg.

"Meet Yorick, the Bionic Skeleton." FDA Kids' Site. (http://www.fda.gov/oc/opa com/Kids/html/yorick_no.1.htm). This site talks about an artificial skeleton called Yorick. It was built to demonstrate many kinds of prosthetics.

"Robots, Robots." Ziggityzoom. (http://www.ziggityzoom.com/characters.php?name=Robot_X). A site about robotics.

"Van Phillips," Lemelson Center Invention Features. (http://www.invention.smithsonian.org/centerpieces/ilives/van_phillips/van_phillips.html). An article for older kids about the inventor of a prosthetic called the Flex-Foot.

Index

Picture Credits

Cover: Courtesy of Touch Bionics
© AFP/Getty Images, 6
AP Images, 17
Carl Court/PA Photos/Landov, 13
Courtesy Lucas Film, 11
Courtesy of Touch Bionics, 4, 5, 14-15, 20 (top), 20 (bottom), 21 (top), 21 (bottom), 22, 25, 27, 28, 30, 31, 34, 37
© Dan McCoy-Rainbow/Science Faction/Corbis. 26
© E.R. Degginger/Alamy, 8

Fabrizio Bensch/Reuters/Landov, 38
© Getty Images, 32
© Helene Rogers/Alamy, 10
© Hulton Archive/Getty Images, 18
© Marco Bularelli/Corbis, 41
© Maxine Hall /Corbis, 7
© McPherson Colin/Corbis Sygma, 36
© Ramin Talaie/Corbis, 23
Shannon Stapelton/Reuters/Landov, 16, 43
© Waltraud Grubitzsch/epa/Corbis, 39

About the Author

Adam Woog is the author of many books for adults, young adults, and children. He lives with his wife and daughter in Seattle, Washington.